My First
RODEO

TIE-DOWN ROPING

Rochelle Groskreutz

www.av2books.com

Step 1
Go to **www.av2books.com**

Step 2
Enter this unique code

YMLEQM3YK

Step 3
Explore your interactive eBook!

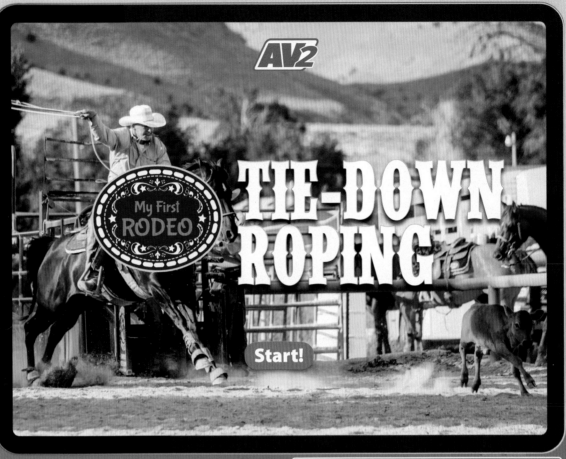

My First RODEO

TIE-DOWN ROPING

Start!

AV2 is optimized for use on any device

Your interactive eBook comes with...

 Read

Audio
Listen to the entire book read aloud

 Videos
Watch informative video clips

 Weblinks
Gain additional information for research

 Try This!
Complete activities and hands-on experiments

 Key Words
Study vocabulary, and complete a matching word activity

 Quizzes
Test your knowledge

 Slideshows
View images and captions

View new titles and product videos at
www.av2books.com

TIE-DOWN ROPING

Contents

The **first** tie-down roping events were held in the **1800s**. They were **friendly contests** between cowboys.

LITTLE VALLEY LAND

BRUN CAT

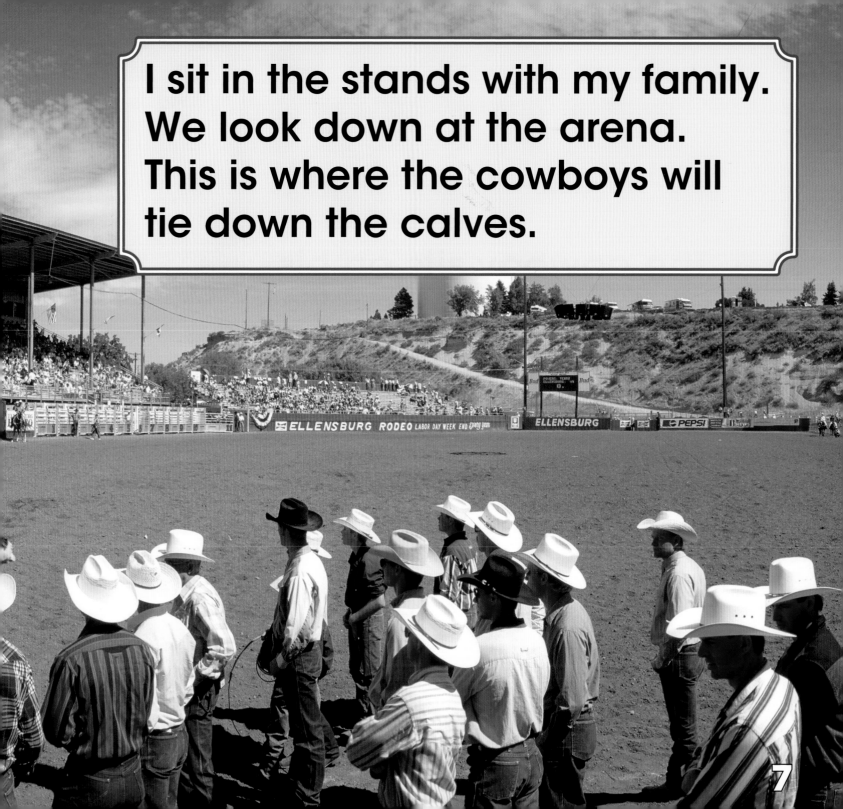

I sit in the stands with my family. We look down at the arena. This is where the cowboys will tie down the calves.

7

The cowboy sits on his horse. They are both ready to go.

The saddle's shape lets the cowboy move freely.

A lasso is used to rope the calf.

Pigging string is used to tie down the calf.

A roping glove keeps the cowboy's fingers safe.

The bridle helps the cowboy control his horse.

9

I see the calf standing in the chute. The cowboy and his horse are in a box beside it.

The cowboy gives a quick nod. The chute opens. The calf runs out.

The calf gets a head start. A barrier rope keeps the cowboy and horse inside the box.

The rope falls. The cowboy charges out on his horse.

10 seconds are added to their time if the cowboy and his horse **cross the barrier** too soon.

The cowboy and his horse chase the calf. The cowboy throws his lasso. He catches the calf.

The horse comes to a stop.
The cowboy jumps off.
He runs to the calf.

The horse waits. It is trained
to keep the lasso tight.

The cowboy flips the calf over. He brings three of its legs together.

The cowboy ties the legs with pigging string. He raises both hands when he is done.

The calf **must stay** tied for **6 seconds**. The ride will not count if it gets up before this.

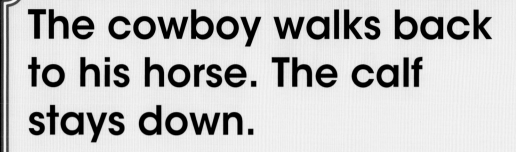

The cowboy walks back to his horse. The calf stays down.

It was a good ride. If no one ropes a calf faster, the cowboy will win first prize.

TIE-DOWN ROPING
FUN FACTS

Roping calves **must weigh** between **220** and **280** **pounds** (100 and 127 kilograms).

Tie-down ropers can make almost **$250,000** in one **year**.

The **first** professional tie-down roping event **for women** was held in **Wyoming** in **2019**.

A **roping calf** can only do about **30 runs** before it is considered too large for the event.

Top tie-down ropers can **rope and tie** a calf in less than **7 seconds**.

A good **roping horse** can cost between **$75,000** and **$100,000**.

KEY WORDS

Research has shown that as much as 65 percent of all written material published in English is made up of 300 words. These 300 words cannot be taught using pictures or learned by sounding them out. They must be recognized by sight. This book contains 78 common sight words to help young readers improve their reading fluency and comprehension. This book also teaches young readers several important content words, such as proper nouns. These words are paired with pictures to aid in learning and improve understanding.

Page	Sight Words First Appearance
4	am, down, first, I, is, my, see, the, this, to
5	between, in, they, were
7	at, family, look, we, where, will, with
8	are, both, go, his, lets, move, on
9	a, helps, keeps, used
10	and, gives, it, opens, out, runs
13	gets, head, if, seconds, soon, start, their, time, too
14	he
17	comes, off, stop
18	before, for, hands, its, must, not, of, over, three, together, up, when
21	back, good, no, one, walks, was
22	almost, can, make, year
23	about, do, large, only, than

Page	Content Words First Appearance
4	rodeo, tie-down roping event
5	contests, cowboys
7	arena, calves, stands
8	horse, saddle, shape
9	bridle, calf, fingers, lasso, pigging string, roping glove
10	box, chute, nod
13	barrier rope
18	legs
21	prize
22	kilograms, pounds, ropers
23	women, Wyoming

Published by AV2
350 5th Avenue, 59th Floor New York, NY 10118
Website: www.av2books.com

Library of Congress Cataloging-in-Publication Data
Names: Groskreutz, Rochelle, author.
Title: Tie-down roping / Rochelle Groskreutz and Heather Kissock.
Description: New York, NY : AV2, [2021] | Series: My first rodeo |
   Audience: Ages 5-8 | Audience: Grades K-1
Identifiers: LCCN 2020004073 (print) | LCCN 2020004074 (ebook) | ISBN
   9781791124083 (library binding) | ISBN 9781791124090 (paperback) | ISBN
   9781791124106 | ISBN 9781791124113
Subjects: LCSH: Calf roping--Juvenile literature. | Rodeos--Juvenile
   literature.

Classification: LCC GV1834.45.C34 G76 2021 (print) | LCC GV1834.45.C34
   (ebook) | DDC 791.8/4--dc23
LC record available at https://lccn.loc.gov/2020004073
LC ebook record available at https://lccn.loc.gov/2020004074

Printed in Guangzhou, China
1 2 3 4 5 6 7 8 9 0 24 23 22 21 20

022020
100919

Project Coordinator: Heather Kissock   Designer: Ana María Vidal

AV2 acknowledges Getty Images, Alamy, Newscom, and iStock as the primary image suppliers for this title.